Praying Together

BOOKS BY CHARLIE AND MARTHA SHEDD

To help you manage your life . . .

The Fat Is in Your Head
Time for All Things: Ten Affirmations for Christian Use of Time
Devotions for Dieters

For young people . . .

The Stork Is Dead
You Are Somebody Special (edited by Charlie Shedd)
How to Know If You're Really in Love

On marriage . . .

Letters to Karen: On Keeping Love in Marriage
Letters to Philip: On How to Treat a Woman
Talk to Me
The Best Dad Is a Good Lover
Celebration in the Bedroom (coauthored with Martha Shedd)
How to Stay in Love (coauthored with Martha Shedd)
Bible Study Together
Praying Together

For parents and grandparents . . .

You Can Be a Great Parent
Smart Dads I Know
A Dad Is for Spending Time With
Grandparents: Then God Created Grandparents and It Was Very Good
Grandparents' Family Book
Tell Me a Story: Stories for Grandchildren and the Art of Telling Them

Ideas for churches . . .

The Exciting Church: Where People Really Pray
The Exciting Church: Where They Give Their Money Away
The Exciting Church: Where They Really Use the Bible
The Pastoral Ministry of Church Officers
How to Develop a Tithing Church
How to Develop a Praying Church

Cassette Resource Kits . . .

Fun Family Forum
Straight Talk on Love, Sex, and Marriage
Good Times With the Bible

Praying Together

Making Marriage Last

Charlie and Martha Shedd

PYRANEE
BOOKS

Zondervan Publishing House
Grand Rapids, Michigan

Praying Together

Copyright © 1987 by Charlie and Martha Shedd

Pyranee Books are published by the Zondervan Publishing House
1415 Lake Drive, S.E., Grand Rapids, Michigan 49506

Library of Congress Cataloging in Publication Data

Shedd, Charlie W.
  Praying together.

  Includes bibliographical references.
  1. Married people—Religious life. 2. Married people—Prayer-books and
devotions—English.
I. Shedd, Martha. II. Title.
BV4596.M3S45 1987   248.3'2'0240655   86-26641
ISBN 0-310-43291-X

Printed in the United States of America

87 88 89 90 91 92 93 / EE / 10 9 8 7 6 5 4 3 2 1

CONTENTS

Acknowledgments

The authors and publisher are grateful to the following publishers for use of the copyrighted materials that are noted in the text:

AMPLIFIED, taken from *The Amplified New Testament.* Copyright © 1954, 1958 by the Lockman Foundation.

GNB, taken from the *Good News Bible, The Bible in Today's English Version.* Old Testament: copyright © 1976 by the American Bible Society; New Testament: copyright © 1966, 1971, 1976 by American Bible Society.

KJV, taken from the *King James Version.*

NEB, taken from *The New English Bible.* Copyright © 1961, 1970 by the Delegates of the Oxford University Press and the Syndics of the Cambridge University Press.

PHILLIPS, taken from J. B. Phillips, *The New Testament in Modern English,* Revised Edition, the Macmillan Company. Copyright © 1958, 1960, 1972 by J. B. Phillips.

RIEU, taken from Emil Victor Rieu, *The Four Gospels.* Copyright © 1953 by Penguin Press.

• • •

C&M indicates the authors' paraphrase.

Basic question for married Christians:

"I'M A CHRISTIAN

YOU'RE A CHRISTIAN

BUT ARE WE CHRISTIANS TOGETHER?"

Chapter I

To Be Absolutely Sure

"What can a couple do to be *absolutely* sure their marriage will last?"

Constantly this same plaintive query continues to surface. It surfaces in our workshops, in personal consultation, over the phone, and by letters beaucoup. Dozens, hundreds, thousands of times we hear it asked, in many versions, against many backgrounds.

There is this one couple in our church who seemed to have a good thing going between them. They even taught our couples' class together for a while. Now, we can hardly believe it! They are getting a divorce and we are all simply stunned. I mean, really in shock about it.

And do you know why?

I think it's because we're scared. What if that happened to us? Most of us think we have a good marriage most of the time, but don't you imagine they must have thought so too?

Well, we talked it over and decided to write you with this one question:

What can a couple do to be *absolutely* sure their marriage will last?

For us there are two answers.

Our earlier book* on Bible study together was answer one for us. Through almost fifty years together we've been sharing the Scriptures with each other. And this is answer two: For almost fifty years we've been learning how to communicate with the Lord in prayer together.

And this is His amazing claim:

The same God who puts out the stars at night

who makes the sun to shine and orders the universe

---

*Available now in paperback is a co-piece to *Praying Together*. *Bible Study Together: Making Marriage Last*, Zondervan, 1987, was published in 1984 under the title *Bible Study in Duet*.

13

That same God will come to live at our address

and in our love together

If we give ourselves to a life of prayer.

Almost everyone we hear on marriage and many of those we read tell us that better communication is the secret to a healthy marriage. They're right. Too many couples we know walk away from their marriages because whatever communication they had was the exchanging of surface data, and the question stands:

> What is the point of establishing channels of communication between husband and wife if there is no life-giving message to fill the channels?*

For us, both Bible study together

and praying together

Become the answers to

communication at its best.

We also believe that for all husbands and wives

everywhere

They are the *absolute* answer

to this oft-repeated question:

"What can a couple do to be *absolutely*

sure their marriage will last?"

---

*From the foreword of *Bible Study Together: Making Marriage Last*, Dr. Eugene Nida, Former Executive Secretary for the United Bible Societies of the World, Consultant for the American Bible Society.

Chapter II

"Coalescing"

One of our favorite words to describe the perfect marriage is "coalesce." The dictionary says that coalescing means "to unite, blend, merge."

All positives; strong, firm feelings. But even the casual observer must sense that true coalescing could almost never be a happening.

Certainly some superb relationships do seem spontaneous. We chanced to be there, here they came—sensational! Sudden harmony! But for the majority of us, love at its best will not be like that.

> Marriage may be "made in heaven" in the original. But the whole deal is more like one of those kits which comes knocked down for putting together. It will take some gluing here, sanding rough spots there, hammering a bit now, filing down the scratches on this side, planing a bit on that side, carving a piece, bending this section slightly, varnishing, backing off for a frequent look, dusting, waxing, polishing, until at last what you have is a thing of beauty and a joy forever.*

Most of us start marriage on the delusion that our coming together will be heaven right now. Special delivery today, or at least tomorrow. Presto-chango, we are on the fast track to paradise.

Then almost before we know it, someone or something changes the music. "Ah Sweet Mystery" fades away, and what are they playing now? "Where Have All the Flowers Gone?"

> How come I never noticed these peculiarities? Your habits, some of your attitudes, certain words you use, certain phrases, the odd way you do things. That tinge of jealousy boxing me in. Your stubbornness and worst of all your stony silence. Wherever are you coming from?

---

*From *Letters to Karen* by Charlie Shedd (Nashville: Abingdon, 1965), p. 23.

Unique report? No. Every husband and every wife who ever said "I do" has heard those sounds. Every marriage counselor has heard them too. In many chambers, down many streets, behind many doors the sound goes on—

"He talks too little."

"She talks too much."

"You've heard of the sphinx? Well, I married it."

"Never a quiet moment. Like Tennyson's brook she babbles on."

"She lives by three slogans: Buy. Buy. Buy."

"You can't believe how tight he is. Won't spend one skinny dime."

"You think he'd ever apologize? Never. Not once would he say, 'I'm sorry.'"

"She never forgets. Always bringing up the past. Throwing the garbage."

"Most of the time I have the feeling he's using me."

"She doesn't really love me. She only loves herself loving me."

"She's never warm."

"He's never home."

On and on and what's the matter? The matter is that same basic flaw. These two have never mastered the art of long-term coalescing.

When can we expect to reach the zenith?* Here again there will be a wide divergence in the answers. For us, zenith one hundred percent must be some time after forty-seven years. For most of us, doesn't the poet say it well,

---

*Dictionaries define "zenith" as "the highest point" . . . "heavenly" . . . "the celestial" . . . "summit" . . . "peak."

"Heaven is not gained in a single bound."

Instead, isn't it more inch by inch, week by week?

One small percentage better this year,

      another percentage and another?

All these years and still we can only say, "Ninety percent of the time our marriage is heaven on earth."

As we look back and evaluate our early years, we can see the percentages clearly now. At the outset, our marriage must have been somewhere near fifty-fifty good and bad. "Sometimes up, sometimes down! Oh yes, Lord."

Today after forty-seven years, honest evaluation of the present gives us ninety percent on the plus side. That other ten percent? On occasion, awful. Why? Because the more we love and the longer we love, the more we hurt when we don't love. Result? The more things go wrong, the more we rush to make them right. Which considered in depth becomes another fine question about love on the upward move—

      Are we increasingly discontented

        with our discontent

      and increasingly grateful

        for every small percentage gained?

One percent improvement, or almost one percent per year, does seem sometimes like progress zero. But take it from a couple who knows because they've been there—the years *are* going to pass some way at some pace. Then wouldn't it be great to look back fifty years from now and say,

      "See how far we've come.

      And here we are still together

Still blending,

Still melding, still coalescing."

That is our experience and this is our witness:

The more we have prayed over the years

The more we have studied our Bibles together

The closer we've come to one-hundred percent

heaven on earth.

So sound that note again! Repeat! One more time!

Christian marriage is for growing in the Lord.

"Growing in the Lord" must have a strange ring to nonbelieving ears. But those of us with faith in our Divine origin know it has to be true. "Growing in the Lord" is the Christian couple's constant challenge, and this should be no surprise to us.

More than one hundred times the Bible talks of growth—growth of the child, the seed, the trees, the church. It also speaks of individual growth, of continually checking for growth, of making certain we are growing. But above all, the admonition is that we must be growing in the Lord. Individually and together, this is our Holy call:

"Speaking the truth in a spirit of love

we grow up in every way to Christ . . .

held together in him."

(Ephesians 4:15)

For the Christian couple this has to be coalescing at its heavenly best.

Chapter III

"Behold, I Stand at the Door"

"Behold, I stand at the door and knock," saith the Lord. "If any man will open the door, I will come in."

Revelation 3:20

It was a great day for us when we caught the meaning of Revelation 3:20. Until then our dominant thought was turned in the wrong direction. We conceived of prayer first as an effort to bring the Lord in. Seeking, pleading, asking, we must draw His attention to our needs.

Then gradually came the light. Prayer, at its finest, is not beating on heaven's door. It is rather opening inner doors to the Lord. Always in the Divine-human encounter, the first move is God's move.

Until the arrival of His Son, mankind had thought of God off there in the distance—Creator, judge, credential-checker. But now came Jesus with an entirely new picture. "Behold," He said, "I stand at the door and knock." Always knocking, always hoping, always ready to enter any door.

Sounds idyllic. We open. He comes. But is it so idyllic? No! Always at the center of our faith is The Cross.

THE CROSS

The Cross means many things, but one thing it means for sure is that God wants His way in our lives. He wants to live in us, think through us, act through us, reshape us. For most of us that means a thorough overhaul. Individually and together there must be some changes made.

The Divine Presence does not come as a courteous guest. He makes demands. He goes through every room, looks under the rugs, opens drawers. Up to the attic, down to the basement, into all the closets and storage places. Everywhere He wants to know, "What's this? What's that?" And if we let

23

Him stay, some things will have to go, some changes will need to be made. Changes in ourselves, changes in attitudes, changes in our relationship to each other.

Small wonder the ancient mystics sometimes talked of "agonizing" in prayer. Prayer with a cross at its heart could never be all gladness and good times.

Why?

Because the first purpose of prayer is not our getting what we want from the Lord. It is first His getting what He wants from us. This will be true for us, both individually and as a couple.

And when we understand that, we find Him leading us straight up the hill to a cross. Yet wherever did we get the idea that marriage must be a posy patch for our enjoyment?

For the Christian couple marriage means the Lord shaping this relationship to His design.

Hard sometimes. Traumatic. But if we do yield ourselves to His shaping, then comes joy we could never know in any other way. And isn't that exactly how it was with Him?

> *"He for the joy that was set before Him endured the cross."*
>
> *(Hebrews 12:2)*

When the human spirit is ready, God enters without
hesitation or waiting. . . . He is no farther away than the door
of the heart. He stands there, lingering, waiting for us to
open the door and let Him in. You need not call to him as if
he were far away, for he waits more urgently than you for the
door to be opened. . . . The opening of the door and his entry
are simultaneous.

Meister Eckhart
1260–1329

Chapter IV

Are We Christians Together?

I am a Christian.

You are a Christian.

But now comes the important question:

Are we blending together with the Lord?

Is ours a Christian marriage?

Our *Fun in Marriage* workshop, session three on "Soul Communication," begins with a questionnaire.

After sessions one and two ("Talk, Talk, Talk"; and "Celebration in the Bedroom"), the mood always changes. It becomes a time for reverence; for going inside to see how we're doing at the core.

Printed here is a copy of that questionnaire on "Soul Communication." We recommend that it be taken individually . . . that you each give a rating to the questions on a separate paper (zero to one hundred, with seventy for passing). A comparison of grades can be exciting. It might also be painful, but whatever it is, the results could be most helpful.

Because this is highly classified data, timing is important. Some days require all the strength we have just to go on breathing. Other times are for the heavies. But for sure, any time is a good time for checking on:

"How am *I* doing that *we* might be doing

better for the Lord?"

SEARCH FOR A BETTER MARRIAGE—SOUL

1. When it comes to vital, livable religion, I rate our marriage overall ____.

2. In theological understanding, early training, and genuine caring for the things of God, I rate myself ____; my mate ____.

3. Our church life together can be rated ____; my own ____; my mate's ____.

4. At the point of sensitivity and service to the needs of other people, I rate my mate ____; myself ____.

5. "I WANT YOU TO BE YOU" . . . "I RESPECT YOUR INDIVIDUALITY" . . . "LET FREEDOM RING." Because God made us unique, these sounds will be heard often in a good marriage. At this point I rate our marriage overall ____; my own attitude ____; my mate's ____.

6. The time I give to Bible reading and study of Scriptures rates ____; my mate's ____.

7. I have my own personal prayer time. Yes ____ No ____

8. My spouse and I pray together regularly. Yes ____ No ____
   I would like to. Yes ____ No ____

9. When it comes to mercy, grace, forgiving, and forgetting, I rate my attitude ____; my mate's ____.

10. If it is true that the family is "the number one theological seminary," for overall relationship to the Lord, including family devotions, I rate our family ____.

Chapter V

Start After
Start After
Start

"I'd rather talk with God alone
    than to talk with God with you."

Most couples who have tried praying together will understand that statement. Praying together has such a pleasant sound, a winsome and amiable ring. "Come, let us be best friends, friends with each other, friends with the Lord." But in actuality the prayer together does not come off like this, not at first.

It didn't for us. Married in our final year at seminary, we were headed for the pastoral ministry. From the beginning we had assumed that we should pray together. Jesus had plenty to say about blind leading blind, and we understood. If we weren't growing spiritually, how could we help our people?

On the wall of our study we had tacked this ancient motto:

> When diving and finding
>
> No pearls in the sea,
>
> Blame not the ocean
>
> The fault is in thee.

So we tried. We tried this, we tried that, we tried and tried and tried. And almost all of our trying was based on a mistaken assumption.

Must We Have Sound?

Wherever did we get the idea that we must pray *aloud* with each other? Is it because our minds are programmed for constant audibles? Television, radio, music, utterance; these we have always with us. Every waking hour, noise. Is this why we fall into the trap of believing that communication can only be vocal?

For whatever reason, all of our experiments were in spoken words, prayer aloud. But no one of our efforts was lasting.

In some way the climate was wrong.

We weren't comfortable. Praying aloud made us nervous.

"Awkward. Embarrassing."

"I have this sneaky feeling I must check everything I'm telling the Lord against 'What will Charlie think?'"

"Suppose Martha doesn't like what I'm about to say. Won't this hurt her feelings?"

That's how it went, start after start after start. And every new beginning was eventually laid low by that same strange label, "I'd rather talk with God alone than to talk with God with you."

Then one year—somewhere in our first five—our relationship came on one of those "no other place to go" emergencies.

What now? If we *could* get through to the Lord together, would He have some answers for us?

We decided on one more try. Only this time we would *not* give up. This time we would find out, "Can prayer together be for real *any* way?" This time we would study prayer. This time we would dig deep in the writings on prayer. We would begin again and keep on beginning and pray for a major breakthrough.

Prayer in Silence

Suddenly there it was—a new approach. Why not start our prayer time with the list of things we'd like to pray about? Then when we had shared enough to understand each other, we would go to the Lord together in silence.

So that's how we did it.

We would sit on our rocking love seat. We would take turns telling each other things we'd like to pray about. Then holding hands we would pray, each in our own way, silently.

34

This was the beginning of prayer together that lasted. Naturally, through the years we've learned to pray in every possible way, including aloud. Anytime, anywhere, every position, every setting, in everyday language. Seldom with "thee" or "thou." Plain talk. Ordinary conversation. We interrupt, we laugh, we argue, we enjoy. We hurt together, cry together, wonder together. Together we tune our friendship to the Friend of friends.

Do we still pray silently together? Often. Some groanings of the spirit go better in the silence.

"I've been feeling anxious lately and I don't know why. Will you listen while I tell you what I can? Then let's pray about the known and unknown in silence."

"This is one of my super days. So good. Yet somehow I can't find words to tell you. Let's thank the Lord together in the quiet."

Negatives, positives, woes, celebrations, shadowy things—all these, all kinds of things we share in prayer. Aloud we share what we can. Without the vocals we share those things not ready yet for words.

Why would this approach have the feel of the real? Almost from the first we knew we'd discovered an authentic new dimension.

In becoming best friends with each other,

we were becoming best friends with the Lord.

And the more we sought His friendship,

the more we were becoming best friends

with each other.

Chapter VI

Why We Don't Stay With It

"When Would We Ever Find Time?"

You want to know why we don't pray together. It's simple. We never find time. We have three teenagers, and can you imagine what that's like? Basketball, soccer, band. Cheerleading, ballet, music lessons, and "Won't you help me with my homework?" Then church activities, choir, and all those youth events for heaven's sake.

But that's not the whole problem. David has done extremely well, and that means long hours, board meetings, big worries. He comes home so tired. Now I've gone back to work part time. I'm an ad executive and I love it, but I come home tired too.

We're trying to stay active in our church. We met at a youth conference and our faith has always been a big thing with us. We used to read the Bible together and pray, and we do intend to get back to it as soon as we can. But right now the term we use for it is "Elijah's whirlwind." And you ask us why we don't pray together.

Well, I want to ask you, "Like when? When would we ever find time?"

• • •

Straight to the target for excuse number one, question one: "When would we ever find time?"

Answer: We never *find* time; we have to *make* time. Time has to be managed. Time has to be scheduled.

By sacred covenant and holy commitment we must pledge to each other, "Everything else comes second to our tuning in upward together."

If the question is not "When do we find time?" but "How do we make time?". . . then, How *do* we make it?

Many answers.

Some prefer morning when the day is fresh. Before

breakfast, after breakfast, "just before we leave for work." How could a couple manage that? "We set our clocks thirty minutes early, and if you knew how we like our sleep, you'd know that takes some doing."

Another husband and wife report their best time for prayer together is immediately after they get home from work. Both employed, they say, "It's a super phase-out of the day's trivia. Gets us ready for a beautiful evening together. It's also sort of a daily re-entry into item one, our soul relationship."

"Right after dinner" . . . "Right after the evening news" . . . "Right before we go to bed" . . . "Right before we fall asleep." We've heard them all, and all good. Any time is a good time so long as it's a good time for this particular couple.

Things Matter More Than People

Reason one, excuse one: Time!

And the second is a first cousin.

Enter this letter from a wondering wife:

> When you married us, you asked us to promise that if we ever even thought of divorce, we'd write you. So I'm writing you, because as much as I hate to tell you, that's what I'm thinking of, and I'm struggling.

> You remember Herb. Anyone could tell by looking at him that success was his middle name, which is exactly where the problem is. Almost from the first he's been saying, "One more big deal, then we'll really live. We'll travel, have fun, enjoy life, be together."

> But every time he gets another big deal, what do you think happens? What happens is that he wants one more big deal. So here I am waiting like I've waited all these years, and the children are growing up, and Herb has hardly noticed, and he certainly doesn't notice how much I'm hurting, and I tell him, but he can't hear me. You know why? He doesn't hear because he doesn't care. All he cares about is one more big deal. I tell you I've talked and begged and prayed and done my best to change what I can in me, but you can only change so much, can't you? When your God-given dignity starts to go, you have to wonder, don't you? Please tell me. Do you know other men like this? Other women who have been through this? And what did they do, and is there anything at all I can do?

• • •

Yes, we've known other men like this. Too many. We've known other women in the same sad trap. What did they do? Some toughed it out. Some didn't. Some joined the madness and almost every time that led to an even sadder sadness. Some said their final good-by. And is there any greater sadness than this—one marriage ended when it might have been mended by one change in the agenda.

But agenda changes are an inside job. If Herb won't change his priorities; if she's already changed to the Lord's limit; then all options have expired, but two:

Stay and keep her hand in The Hand of The Lord alone.

Go and keep her hand in The Hand of The Lord alone.

A sinister mindset, this obsession, "Things are number one. Things matter more than people." Even more sinister than "busyness." Like termites this one eats away at the heart of a relationship until finally all the fibers are gone.

· · ·

For some saving contemplation—

Is there even a slight possibility

   that "things are number one"

      might eventually destroy our marriage?

If so, what changes should we be making right now?

Lack of Mutual Respect

Fade-away number three comes clear in these letters:

You want to know why my wife and I don't pray together
or study the Bible together? Or even why I don't go to
church with her anymore? It's that group she got into two
years ago, that's why. You can't believe what they've done to
Sally. They've taken a perfectly wonderful woman and
changed her into a spiritual snob. They call themselves "The
Higher Ground." I call them "The phony cousins of Jesus."
They think they are so perfect, so faultless, they look down
their noses at everyone who isn't one of them.

• • •

Pomposity of any kind, large, small,

spoken, silent, without fail

this is another prime destroyer

of spiritual marriage.

From a pastor's wife:

My husband is a minister, very successful. He is also very
formal, and that's the problem. Many times we've started
praying together, but he insists on bringing his formality into
our prayer life. Me? From the time I was little, I've prayed in
such simple language. So here we are, me with my childhood
ways and him with his "thee's" and "thou's" plus theological
terms I don't even understand. Somehow I get the feeling
that he feels he's way out there ahead of me. I'd like to have a
better relationship with the Lord with him. Yet that's the way
it is and what can we do with this problem?

• • •

Another imperative for prayer together—mutual respect.
Oneness of the highest kind can never be achieved without
it. We must say to each other and mean it:

I may be different from you,

    but I'm not better.

I may know more than you know about my things,

    but you know more than I know about yours.

        Let us honor each other's uniqueness

        As we honor the Lord together.

Fear

"Where would we ever find time?"

Things matter more than people

A lack of mutual respect

Reasons why our prayer life slips away.

Reason four is FEAR!

"Marjorie thinks I am so fine, and a part of me likes that. But then I ask myself what if she knew everything I'm thinking? How would she feel about me then?"

"Do you think it's important to tell all? I'm afraid praying with Bruce would eventually lead to total honesty and it makes me nervous to even think about that. Would he still love me if he knew everything?"

"We've started praying together many times, but we've never kept it going. Of course we made excuses, but I wonder if the real reason is that it's so scary to be completely open. If we aren't completely open, prayer is a little bit deceitful, isn't it? I think that's how it's been with us. We've begun praying together many times, but then when we come to one of those sensitive places, it seems like one of us backs away."

• • •

What can a couple do when the "classified" data begins to surface and their prayer life makes them nervous?

Answer straight from the soul of a grateful husband:

I think one of the greatest days in our marriage was when Elizabeth Ann told me, "You can tell me anything you're thinking; anything you've done; anything you wish you could do. Tell me your ideas, your fantasies, your mistakes, your dreams, your finest thoughts, your worst, your sins, anything. You tell me and I will only love you more, because I'll know you better."

Then after the report of those high notes, he adds:

Now why would a man ever be unfaithful to a woman like that?

This is GRACE in action, and it is one all-important ingredient for praying together. Never earned, only given—free. That's what it says in the official theological definition of grace. "Grace is the free, unmerited love and favor of God."

BLESSED IS THE COUPLE

WHO BY ANY MEANS WILL

EXTEND TO ONE ANOTHER

GOD'S AMAZING GRACE

THEIRS WILL ONE DAY

BE THE PERFECT LOVE

THAT CASTS OUT FEAR

How does Grace cast out fear in marriage? Grace casts out fear in marriage because we have enabled our mate to be completely honest.

Honesty is important in itself and also for two great by-products: (1) humility, called the queen of the virtues because it mothers all the rest and keeps them from corruption and (2) the ability to be yourself . . . the relief in returning to oneself is almost incredible . . . the blessed, blessed freedom, the release and joy of not having to maintain a front, not having to curry favor, not having to fool anyone! The clear, unshifting gaze and the steady nerves! This is worth working for!

Thomas Powers, *First Questions in the Life of the Spirit*, p. 9, Harper & Brothers, 1959.

Chapter VII

How to Keep It Going

We meet many interesting people on our beach. Friendly, unfriendly, awed, bored, happy, sad. Then there are those extra specials like the "small girl with a bottle."

"Look," she said, "I'm taking the ocean home."

Winsome moment, yet we knew and she would know later, no one takes the ocean home. Not in one small bottle. Not in any way.

As we muse on our little friend, we get the feeling, "Here is a parable of prayer."

Even after centuries of writers writing, after millions of seekers seeking, students studying—still all the knowledge of all the students, all of the wisdom of the scholars—isn't all of it all together like one small bottle of ocean water? Still out there is the real ocean, vast, boundless, infinite.

So with prayer. For centuries and forever, wave after wave, and never an end to the learning.

Did the Apostle mean something like this when he said there are twelve gates to the Holy City? Or if he was thinking of prayer, wouldn't he have said twelve million times twelve million?

Nobody has ever even approached all the gates. Nobody knows all the roads. Nobody has all the answers. And how could we? The more we pray, the more we know what the mystics mean by their quaint phrase, "Many and myriad are the ways of prayer."

This phrase appears often in the language of spiritual pilgrims. We like it. It is a needed reminder that other gates might be every bit as authentic as our own. But here is another exciting fact: The gates we find for ourselves may be every bit as authentic as other people's gates. We must never let others discourage our experiments or put us down or call us off our own discoveries.

In this chapter we present certain approaches to prayer and methods of prayer we've discovered for ourselves. Some of these are oldies, truths others knew long before we heard of them. Then there are those we invented for ourselves, innovations just for us as needed.

Still the Wisdom Writer says, "There is no new thing under the sun" (Ecclesiastes 1:9). Had he been living now, would he have said that?

What does it matter whether he tells it like it is, or was, or will be forever? Isn't this what really matters—that we, in our praying, should be open to the heavenly revelations for us?

Following now are some of the techniques, old and new, that have served as aids in our prayer life. Each of the approaches presented here has been tried, tested, used, and re-used. Each has brought new blessings, positives for our prayer together.

First Thoughts

How am I doing with this admonition of 1 Timothy 2:1?

"First of all, then, I urge that petitions,

prayers, requests, and thanksgiving be offered."

(GNB)

Report from one *Fun in Marriage* workshop. The question for discussion now was, "What do we think about first on awakening?"

"You want the truth? When I first wake up, I'm too stupid to think of anything."

"Where did I leave my cigarettes?"

"The weather. Too hot. Too cold. Too wet. Too dry. Why should my first thoughts be negative?"

"My wife is up before I am, so she wakes me. I know it sounds weird, but my first thought is, 'Why is this woman plaguing me?'"

"I rush for the morning paper. First thought? What did the stock market do yesterday?"

"If you feel like I do when you wake up, you'd think you deserve a medal if you refrained from hitting someone."

Both Old and New Testaments point to the importance of our early-morning thoughts:

"Early will I seek Thee."

"Those that seek me early shall find me."

"And in the morning long before daylight, Jesus got up and went out to a deserted place, and there he prayed."

Almost without exception praying people say this is true: What we think at the outset of our day will make a difference in how we handle that day's happenings. Morbid leads to the morbid. Gladness ushers in more gladness.

This has been our experience. If we discipline ourselves to pray first, our day does go better. But the same daily discipline also affects our long-term prayer life.

It is almost as though we hear the Lord saying,

"You give prayer top priority in your day,

I will help you keep it top priority

through the years."

Such top-priority thinking of the Lord does not come at a bargain price. This is a discipline. And for starters is there any finer Scripture verse than that familiar affirmation of the Psalmist?

"This is the day the Lord has made.

We will rejoice and be glad in it."

(Psalm 118:24)

The sign on our printer's wall read "PF." Nothing more. Large sign. White sheet. White frame. Two big black letters: "PF."

When we asked, "Why the PF?" he explained, "The meaning is PRAY FIRST. I put it there, because I'm trying to break old habits. My natural tendency seems to be to think about me first and all my problems. Worry first, fuss first, panic first, blow up first, act first. But now that I've become a Christian, I'm trying to live by The Book."

PRAY FIRST!

Javelin Prayers

The saints have an interesting term for flashing our thoughts upward. They call it "javelin prayer."

The Bible is replete with this kind of praying, and who of us hasn't done it? Especially in emergencies we pray javelin prayers. Sudden danger, catastrophe, calamity, pain, bad news, storm signals without and within . . .

"Oh God!"

"Lord, help me!"

"Please! Please! Please!"

"Bless him!"

"Bless you!"

"Heal me!"

"Protect her!"

Yet this is only one small part of javelin praying at its best. When we decide to make prayer top priority on our agenda, a fine thing happens. Each day all day seems to be filled with opportunity for the quick upward thrust.

The telephone rings, and who is this? The good news we've been awaiting? Friend? Foe? Someone between the plus and minus? An unknown?

Haven't we done a good thing when we use the phone as a call to prayer? "Bless whoever it is." "Lord, speak through me."

Such prayer does more than help us keep our equilibrium. It blesses others. Our Lord did say He could bless others through us. Why not through us via the telephone?

Other sounds too can be reminders of another moment for prayer.

The sirens: police, fire, ambulance . . .

"May they feel you near."

Airplanes overhead . . .

"Keep them safe."

The doorbell, a knock, the cry of a child . . .

"Use me, Lord."

The chime of a clock . . .

"Thank you, for your gift of minutes and hours."

First Timothy 2:3 says of its call to "prayer, petition, intercession" . . . "Such praying is good and right, and it is pleasing and acceptable to God, our Savior" (AMPLIFIED).

Most of us need all the help we can get to change our prayer life from "me, me, me" to the higher forms of intercession.

Promise:

When we develop the art of javelin prayer

we will know "Such praying *is* good and right."

Good for us.

Good for others.

Good for the known and unknown.

Good and right too for the Lord,

"pleasing and acceptable to Him."

Prayer for Remembering Names

On television recently we saw an amazing performance. Some memory expert was ushered into the studio with thirty strangers. Row by row the Master of Ceremonies introduced each person. Name, where they were from, and what they did for a living.

Then our hero proceeded, row by row, to repeat each name. First name, last name, hometown, occupation. No mistakes.

How did he do it?

"Association," he said. "Blue necktie, white hat, bright lipstick, horn-rimmed glasses, gray hair, etcetera." Unbelievable. Especially unbelievable with so many gray heads, several horn-rimmed glasses, and ever so much bright lipstick.

"How can I remember names?

I don't have much trouble recognizing faces, but I

can't seem to recall who this is."

These are common complaints, and all of us must have our own version of the problem along with solutions. *We* have *our* own version of how to remember names—javelin prayer.

We meet someone new. We pray, "Lord, bless Mike Martin, Mary Jean Johnson, Tom, Bob, Susan, Jane." Almost one hundred percent of these people we will remember by name. Why? Our secular psychologist friends say, "Clever mental trick." But isn't there something more happening here? The Christian believes that we are all related in the Lord. Then why not this explanation of a javelin prayer for remembering names?

He relates us,

> not only for this moment,

> but for moments to come

> when we meet each other again.

Foolproof? No. Dependable? Yes, if we remember the javelin prayer. Unbelievable? Not for the believer. Scripture says,

> "All things cohere in him." (Colossians 1:17 MOFFATT)

For us javelin prayer to remember names has become one more witness of this truth—

> There is a heavenly network

> and we are all related in Him.

The Bible admonishes us to remember one another before the Lord. Couldn't this also mean to remember one another's names?

Celebration of Life's Goodness

What is the highest form of prayer?

From one of our most mature praying friends:

"My highest form of prayer is simply three words:

THANKYOU. THANKYOU. THANKYOU."

Prayer for ourselves—good. Prayer for others—one step up. But haven't we reached an even higher level when we move from "What have you done for me lately?" to "Thank you, Lord, for all you've done."

Important question for any couple:

Is the tone of our marriage

negative _____ positive _____

downbeat _____ upbeat _____

If the tone does need re-doing, how can it be changed? One answer is for husband or wife or both together to learn one thousand different ways to pray, "Thank you, Lord. Thankyou. Thankyou. Thankyou."

Knee praying is almost a lost art in today's Christian homes. We've quit asking those couples who do pray together, "How often do you pray on your knees?" And the reason we quit asking is to avoid the put-down answer, "Never."

But on those rare occasions when someone in our workshops gives witness to praying on their knees, we find their report is exactly like ours. "Knee praying brings a contribution no other kind of praying brings."

Chapter VIII

Word Focusing

Among the innovative approaches to prayer none has done more for us than Word Focusing.* It is based on Jesus' promise in Matthew 6:22, "If therefore thine eye be single, thy whole body shall be full of light."

"Singling the eye" in prayer calls for serious mental discipline. But like so many things in the spiritual life, after the discipline comes pure enjoyment—plus new appreciation of words and the language in general—plus fresh insights into the mind of our mate—plus a sorting out of things in our own mind that need adjustment—plus a deeper relationship with each other—plus a purer oneness together with the Lord—plus the ever-growing appreciation that He does want us to be joyful. "These things have I spoken to you," He said, "that my joy may be in you, and that your joy may be full" (John 15:11 RSV).

Far back in the Middle Ages there were groups who called themselves Contemplatives. They spent one hundred percent of their time concentrating on spiritual things. Their procedure was to take a single phrase and repeat it constantly:

"Thou art my all in all."

"In Him is our peace."

"Praise His Holy name."

These and other phrases opened up new roads to God for them. That's what they claimed, and we believe their claim. We believe it because we tried it, and it worked for us.

---

*Word Focusing was described at length in two previous publications, both out of print. *Word Focusing: A New Way to Pray*, Upper Room, and *Getting Through to the Wonderful You*, Revell, 1976. In each of these books we included additional words and texts that have been especially helpful to our prayer together. Word Focusing as a spiritual practice adapts itself to personal prayer. Families and groups have found it useful, too.

Generally, words we find for ourselves will be most enlightening. However, for those who wish them, an extensive list of both words and texts are available from the authors. Write Charlie and Martha Shedd, c/o Zondervan Corporation, 1415 Lake Drive, S.E., Grand Rapids, Michigan 49506.

Then another wonderful thing happened. We discovered that sometimes focusing on a single word would put us in touch with The Inner Presence.

Various approaches to meditation have run the gamut in our day. From ultra popular to ultra collapse, they come and go. One reason for their passing, we think, is that many of them aim to empty the mind. In Word Focusing we are doing the opposite. We are asking The Inner Presence to fill our minds with His spirit.

This is the *how* of Word Focusing:

- We begin by selecting a word from our Bible reading. In our morning quiet time a single word leaps out at us. It stands there on some mental road demanding our attention.

- When we have chosen a word to incorporate in our prayer life, we look it up in various dictionaries. Amazing how different dictionaries provide different shades of meaning to a single word.

- We agree that in our quiet time we will try to "single" our minds on the chosen word.

- Then we will retain this word until it has accomplished its purpose in us.

- We ask the Lord to apply it to our lives where needed.

- Many times during the day we concentrate on our word. When we are together, we exchange

ideas and what the word has
meant ... how it blessed us ...
what new meanings came to us
and how these can apply to our
relationship. All of which, it is
easy to see, will lead us again to
those three most important words
in any marriage: talk, talk, talk.

● How long do we continue our use
of a single word? It might be one
day, one week or two, a month. So
long as it continues to provide
new insights, we continue with
this word.

● ● ●

Suppose our word is *patience.* One morning in our quiet
time it has come alive for one of us. Reading again in the
New Testament, there it is, "For ye have need of patience"
(Hebrews 10:36). How right can You be, Lord! We need it
badly. So we write down the verse on a slip of paper where
we can refer to it often. (Eventually, of course, the slip gives
way to memory; we learn this verse by heart.)

Our second move is to the dictionary—Patience: "1.
Possessing or demonstrating quiet, uncomplaining endur-
ance under distress, longsuffering. 2. Tolerant, tender,
forbearing. 3. Capable of tranquilly awaiting results."

Having pondered the Bible verse, then having seen it
through the light of several dictionaries, we now make this
word a focal point of our meditating.

All this is no panacea. We still lose patience, blow up, say
things we shouldn't say. What do we do? We pray:

Lord, I need your holy patience.

Control this eager beaver in my soul.

How can one heart like mine hold enough patience

for all these problems, big and little?

Answer, straight from the Source: "It can't. But Christ living in us can."

And when we do let Him live in us, He does fill the gaps in our patience with His patience. He can do what we cannot do as individuals and as couples.

· · ·

Again:

We select a word from Bible reading.

We study its dictionary meaning.

We ponder.

We ask the Lord to apply it where we need it.

We exchange ideas . . . talk, talk, talk.

We continue the word as long as it continues
    blessing our love.

· · ·

Here now are some of our favorite words. With the first group we have included text, dictionary definition, and a prayer. Then comes a list of words, with texts. These we include for those who wish to experiment with Word Focusing. In praying together, for us there has been no finer way to reach the deeps.

ABUNDANCE

"And God is able to provide you with every blessing in abundance, so that you may always have enough of everything and may provide in abundance for every good work."
2 Corinthians 9:9 (RSV)

• • •

Abundance: an ample quantity . . . relative degree of plentifulness . . . full supply.

• • •

Prayer:

Lord, why do we fuss so much about Your goodness

running out before it gets to us?

Why do we worry that we may be shortchanged

Or miss our share of treasures from

Your storehouse?

Have we been straining for things instead of

reaching for you?

Help us to exchange our poverty complex for

an abundance complex.

Teach us to move our eyes from intake to outgo—

We know that when we give what we should,

You will provide what we need.

We know too that You can provide what

other people need through us.

Write it on our hearts:

You are the Lord of "ample quantity, plenty,

full supply."

Thank you for choosing us as your trustees.

MATURITY

"Therefore, let us leave the elementary doctrine of Christ and go on to maturity ..."

Hebrews 6:1 (RSV)

. . .

Mature: highly developed or advanced in intellect, moral qualities, outlook ... perfected, detailed ... being completed or ready.

. . .

Prayer:

Lord, do you need us on a higher plane?

Teach us to open our minds for fresh thoughts.

Grow us up.

Expand our understanding.

. . .

Check questions for frequent review:
1. Can we increasingly tell the important from the unimportant?
2. Are we growing in the wisdom to keep silent when we should?
3. Is it easier now for us to apologize when we are wrong?
4. Do we have new courage to stand for what we believe?
5. Are we more able to pray for those who do not like us?
6. Are we continually moving to higher levels, deeper places, in our prayer life?
7. Together are we "leaving the elementary doctrine of Christ and going on to maturity"?

INFLUENCE

"A wise man is esteemed for being pleasant; his friendly words add to his influence."

Proverbs 16:21 (MOFFATT)

. . .

Influence: an emanation of spiritual or moral force . . . the act or power of producing an effect without apparent exertion of force . . . changing the nature of . . .

. . .

The writer of Proverbs opens a two-way road for us here. The things we see, voices we hear, thoughts we entertain—these will influence us. But that's not all. Our words, our acts, our touch, our thoughts—all these, for good or bad, will influence others.

. . .

Prayer:

Lord, we can hardly believe it—

We are a part of Your influence.

Help us to remember that others are reading You

by reading us.

Filter the forces flowing into our hearts that

we may be the finest kind of influence for You.

COURTESY

"Finally, be ye all of one mind, having compassion one of another, love as brethren . . . be courteous."

1 Peter 3:8 (KJV)

• • •

HEALTH

"Never pride yourself on your own wisdom, revere the Eternal and draw back from sin; that will mean health for your body and fresh life to your frame."

Proverbs 3:7, 8 (MOFFATT)

• • •

LIGHT

"Then Jesus again addressed them saying, 'I am the light of the world; he who follows me will never walk in darkness, he will enjoy the light of life.'"

John 8:12 (MOFFATT)

• • •

SAFETY

"And you will have confidence, because there is hope; you will be protected and take your rest in safety."

Job 11:18 (RSV)

Some time ago we were in an airport making a phone call. At the phone next to us an old man—very old—was looking through the directory. Only he wasn't looking like we would look, and not like most people. Instead he had rolled up a piece of paper, shaping it like a funnel. He pointed the narrow end right down to the page, then peered through the larger opening. Watching us watching him, he smiled and said, "Ever try it? Sometimes when you cut out all the other print, you can see what you're looking for real plain."

"If therefore thine eye be single, thy whole body shall be full of light."

Chapter IX

Blessings and Gifts

*"Set your heart first on his kingdom
and his goodness, and all these
things will come to you as a matter
of course."*

Matthew 6:33 (PHILLIPS)

In this section we present the beautiful happenings of forty years at prayer. Insights, lessons, challenges, plus gentle nudges and firm warnings for correction. Some of these have come accompanied by a heavy knock, others on padded feet. Yet even the flashes of new light most often seem to follow months and years of setting our hearts "first on his kingdom."

That does seem to be exactly what Matthew 6:33 means in its original. The *Amplified New Testament* reads, "But seek for (aim at, strive after) first of all his kingdom and his righteousness (his way of doing)."

Husbands and wives creating a togetherness through prayer soon discover the reality of this translation. Here we are again at that inevitable fact—

"His way of doing" is never a happening

in intimate relationships.

The building of any Christlike union is

a creation.

This section reports on certain blessings and gifts we have experienced. Each blessing, each gift comes to focus in a Scripture passage that has brought special meaning to us. In our format here each Scripture is followed by a meditation for couples. Then come questions for discussion and a prayer for praying together.

BLESSING OF THE HAPPY SURPRISES

*"Eye hath not seen nor ear heard,
neither have entered into the heart of
man the things God has prepared for
them that love him."*

1 Corinthians 2:9 (KJV)

We have heard this verse preached or seen it frequently in Christian literature. And almost always these thoughts focus on heaven. That's good. We need now and then to consider the hereafter.

Yet for couples in the duet of prayer, 1 Corinthians 2:9 will bring other meanings. One of these is sure to be:

The more we tune to heavenly wavelengths

The more God's heavenly blessings come.

Here, hereafter, and in between.

In countless serendipities and unexpected surprises they come. This Monday, next Thursday, any day, any moment, now.

Did you ever dial a number, pick up the phone, and there was no ring? Why? Because the person you were dialing was dialing you.

The Bible tells us that God loves us so much He is constantly dialing us.

In our Old Testaments sometimes we hear the ringing far away. But as we put our ear down to New Testament writings, the sound comes loud and clear:

"I'm thinking of you, caring

for you. Calling today to say I love you."

Questions:

What unusual happening lately in our love could only have been "prepared by the Lord" because He loves us?

As we ponder the happy surprises of our life together, when have the showers of blessing most often come?

Would there be even more happy surprises if we developed the art of listening more together? Exciting thought, isn't it, 1 Corinthians 2:9? Imagine all the wonderful things our Lord could do to us, for us, through us if we would love Him as He loves us.

Prayer: Lord, when we stay on your line, you do have such a thrilling way of making life good, making life interesting. What an amazing God you are. Even when we leave off calling you, you never quit calling us. Thank you. Thank you. Thank you.

Amen

APPRECIATION OF THE LITTLE THINGS

"Consider the lilies ... how they grow."

Matthew 6:28, Luke 12:17 (KJV)

On a recent trip, our road took us over another detour. Always the detours. Sooner, later, and mostly too often, there they are—those temporary delays. Bridge out . . . road repairs . . . "Please be patient, we're doing this for you."

On this particular day as we drove along scolding our luck, we came on a country blessing. Another vignette for warm recall.

There in the front yard of their home was an elderly couple teaching their newborn calf to drink from a bottle. Grandpa holding calf on wobbly legs. Grandma tipping bottle. So we parked, watched, and joined in the great good time. Laughter. Fun. Togetherness at its best.

One more of God's special gifts—Each new scene brings to mind new musings. Where was the mother cow? Did she reject her baby? Had she run out of milk? Was this a twin? Triplet? How many times over the years had these senior citizens been through this scene together?

"Consider the lilies."

Consider the pelicans flying in formation. Consider the smell of dinner cooking. Consider the laugh of a baby. Consider our granddaughter's dimples. Consider how many million little things we too often overlook.

• • •

Exercise for a biblical good time:

We will make a trip through the Gospels with this one

question: How many items that we generally overlook did Jesus use for a lesson?

Red sky at night ... Red sky in the morning

A fallen sparrow

Fish for breakfast

One lost coin

An ear of corn

Water for washing feet

Needles and rope and a homely camel

Was there ever a greater appreciator of the common things than our Lord? Then doesn't this make sense? The prayer that Christ-centers our relationship will result in many more little blessings we could be sharing together.

"Today I saw something I'd never noticed before.

Let me tell you about it. Let us now 'Consider the lilies.'"

Prayer: Lord, you were so alive to the world around you, to places, to people, to things. Make us more sensitive. Whenever, wherever, alone, and especially together teach us the fine art of Christ-like response to that wonderful world of the commonplace.

Amen

THE GIFT OF LISTENING

Eight times Jesus said, "Those who have ears to hear, let them hear" (Matthew 11:25, Matthew 13:9, Matthew 13:43, Mark 4:9, Mark 4:23, Mark 7:16, Luke 8:8, Luke 14:35).*

Modern translations open up new vistas:

"Be careful how you listen." Mark 4:23 (PHILLIPS)

"The man who has ears to hear should use them." Matthew 13:9 (PHILLIPS)

"Take note of what you hear." Mark 4:23 (NEB)

"Give your minds to what you hear." Mark 4:23 (RIEU)

"Be sure you really listen." Mark 4:23 (C&M)

• • •

From a wife: "Every time I start some deep discussion, my husband does the disappearing act. I know the man is busy. I know he has a lot of things on his mind. I know he's under terrific pressure right now. I know he needs quiet and time to be alone. But what about my pressures, my needs? If just once he'd sit down and listen, I mean listen all the way through to my real feelings."

From a husband: "I call my wife 'motor mouth.' She never stops talking long enough to hear what I'm saying, and certainly never long enough to catch my train of thought."

---

*The "principle of escalating attention" is described at length in *Bible Study Together*, p. 126.

Why are so many of us so much like this? Nobody knows all the answers, but we know one for sure. With us it's plain old selfishness. "I, me, my, mine."

Some things, the Bible says, "go not out but by prayer." Breaking up our selfishness is another of the miracles that will only come as we turn to the Lord together. If we ask Him, He will bring his hammers to break these hard crusts of our self-concentration. Then when this painful work is over, in place of the broken pieces, he leaves another blessing. He teaches us to genuinely care what our mate is feeling, thinking, saying.

Groanings of the Spirit

Some feelings we feel, but can't express. This must be what the Bible means by "groanings of the spirit." And when they come in our prayers together, these are ultra-sensitive moments. Now what will we do? Will we turn away? Respond with some unfeeling remark? Or will we use this occasion to practice what psychologists call "listening with the third ear"?

For the Christian this kind of listening is no mystery. Our Lord has promised that if we let Him, He will live in us and do what we can't do. He *will* listen through us. He *will* improve our caring. He *will* tune our ears to the heard and unheard.

Mysterious, marvelous gift of His Spirit.

If ever one bit of Christly advice is worth a ton, this is it:

"Be sure you really listen."

• • •

For listening, really listening, on a scale of zero to one hundred, I think our relationship deserves a grade of _____.

My grade _____ Yours _____

Prayer: Lord Jesus, sometimes only you can stop the flow of our words. Help us to know that what the other person says matters more to them than what we say. Break our selfish preoccupation. Teach us how to really listen, listen all the way.

Amen

DELAYED BLESSING FROM THE
HARD THINGS

> *"And we know that all things work
> together for good to them that love
> God."*
>
> *Romans 8:28 (KJV)*

"All God's chillun' got trouble these days."

Every couple we know has experienced disappointment. Every couple we know has been hurt. Every couple we know has experienced some valleys.

So for all of us there will be these crucial questions.

What do we do when the shadows come? Will we clam up, grow stoic, refuse to discuss our pain? Jam our hours and minutes full to keep from thinking in the dark blues? Can we party it away? "Mix me another drink"—Turn the agony to liquid? Depress it? Fuzzy it some other way? Could there be comfort with a mate more understanding? A different partner? Would they have a balm for the aching?

All these questions sound so morbid, so unrealistic. Yet how many couples in any circle of friends did crash on the wave of some major calamity? Answer: Many too many!

Comes now the old country sage with his whimsy:

"Same fire hardens the egg and melts the butter."

Why?

One answer has to be communication or the dearth thereof. The agony was never shared in toto. Bits and pieces maybe, an effort or two, surface thoughts. But then came those familiar fears, the old tremors. "He wouldn't understand." "She'd only preach." So without knowing what we've done, we blur it. And for the Christian couple this will never do.

There is no other healing, no other way than talk, talk, talk; plus listen, listen, listen. Sharing and sharing some more and sharing it all is the only answer. And for those who dare to begin, this is another of God's great gifts—the more we share what we can share now, the more He gives us to share in our next exchange. On and on forever, that's how it goes. For years it goes on like this until we experience another mystery. Our talk, talk, talk with each other to the maximum has led us to maximum union with the Lord.

Romans 8:28 has been called "the Bible's most positive promise." To which the experienced Christian can only say "Amen." Yet when we go behind the positive promise for a second look, we see a somber negative.

Romans 8:28 does not tell us that all things are good. Some of our happenings are bad, very bad. That being true, our question tends to be, "Can't we buy insurance anywhere to protect us from calamity?"

To which the answer is forever, "We cannot." There is no absolute safeguard, no escape, no guarantee. What Romans 8:28 does give us is not *insurance,* but *assurance.*

• • •

Questions:

What was the hardest thing that ever happened

in our marriage?

Has some good come out of it?

How?

• • •

Prayer: Lord, we do believe that nothing can ever defeat you, nothing! Help us to remember that here in our valley we draw close together. Help us to discuss our hurt together fully. Then teach us how together we can give it to you. Take our sorrow. Thank you for working it into your pattern for good.

Amen

THE GIFT OF CERTAINTY

"Hereby do we know that we know."

1 John 2:3 (KJV)

How can we know absolutely?

First John 2:3 tells us that "we can know we know" by obedience. One translation gives us this condition: "Knowing that we know comes from observing and practicing his teaching" (AMPLIFIED).

Promise: Those who will pray together for an extended period (try twenty years, or forty) will be given the heavenly gift of certainty, the Lord's certainty.

When we have prayed together for specific guidance, when we both come to the same conclusion, we can know this is what God wants for us.

From our years of prayer together we can attest to the truth of 1 John 2:3. We can also attest to three more truths from that truth:

1. If we do what He shows us today He will show us more tomorrow.

2. In our individual meditations it is imperative that we discuss together before too long whatever insight has been given us individually.

3. This teaching of 1 John is true in reverse. If one of us thinks we have an answer and we rush to do it right now without positive feelings from the other, we may be headed for disaster.

• • •

For discussion:

Would we be more likely to *know* what God wants for us if we prayed together and discussed our problems more?

Prayer: Thank you, Lord, that with all
the things you have to attend,
you still have time for us.
Help us to be so effective in
our prayers that we know what
you want and what you need.
Then help us to be effective in
the doing of your will.

Amen

THE GIFT OF SIMPLICITY

"Do it with simplicity."

Romans 12:8 (KJV)

On the desk in our writing room there is a simple three-word motto. Above the sink in our kitchen, the same three words. We see it also on the chest in our bedroom and on the bathroom mirror. In our woodworking shop and on the dashboard of our car, there too these three words:

REDUCING OUR MULTIPLICITY

It's an ancient phrase from the distant past, which we discovered first in our reading of some long-gone mystic. And the more we center these words in our minds, the more they ask some telling questions:

Why do we tend so much to major in the minors?

Why are we so caught up in the muchness and

the manyness of our world

and other people's doings?

A wise old teacher told us, "There are three secrets to great teaching. They are, in fact, three secrets to greatness in almost anything; and these are the three secrets"—

Keep it simple!

Keep it simple!

Keep it simple!

For pondering together:

Where in our lives do we need to reduce our multiplicity?

• • •

Prayer: Lord, here we are in the trivia, fragmented, crowded by people and things and stuff. Teach us to be good sorters, good putters away, good at discerning the important from the unimportant. Today, Lord, teach us to keep it simple.

Amen

THE GIFT OF ADVENTURE

*"So that we too might habitually live
and behave in newness of life."*

Romans 6:4 (AMPLIFIED)

One of the deadliest enemies to love at its growing best has to be boredom.

Boredom with people

Boredom with places

Boredom with activities

Boredom with our job

Boredom with each other

Why so often do we tend to interpret faith as resistance to change?

The poet puts it well:

Our fathers ruled the roost

nineteen hundred years or so;

And to every new proposal

they have always answered "No."

Do we? Or is there in our lifestyle enough of the patriarch's touch: "He went, not knowing whither" (Hebrews 11:8)?

In our years together this has been another mighty gift of prayer—the courage to

experiment with new approaches,

move to new terrain,

launch out.

It does take courage to pray for newness of life. So we find ourselves praying, "Lord, show us your will." But when we examine this prayer in honesty, we know we've included a hooker. And the hooker is that we really mean, "Lord, show us your will so we can decide whether we like what you show us."

It's an ever-expanding verse, Romans 6:4, calling us to honesty without the hooker.

Crucial question:

Are we honest enough,

daring enough to pray and mean it—

> Lord, show us where you want us to change. And this is our pledge: If you show us, we will do what you show us. Keep us habitually living and behaving in newness of life.
>
> Amen

THE BLESSING OF SEX AT ITS MAXIMUM*

> "... they twain shall become one
> flesh."
>
> Genesis 2:24

Prayer of a Happy Wife

It was a *Fun in Marriage* workshop. Midwest setting, church sponsored. We were into the section on "Body Communication" and from many came the usual plaintive wailing: "If only we had a better sex life, everything would be so fine." Over and over and over we hear it!

> "I grew up in a vacuum. Even in junior high when I needed to know things, everybody around me just plain played deaf and dumb. Nobody taught me anything."

"You're lucky. In our family they taught us, but they taught us all wrong. The big idea was this stuff is really bad."

> "Why is my wife so uptight about variety in sex?"

And on and on until one wife stood up for her announcement, "I didn't have any help either. But then something happened that changed our sex life, and I'd like to tell you about it."

Full attention now.

---

*See *Celebration in the Bedroom* (Waco, Tex.: Word Inc., Second Edition, 1985).

"Always my husband has wanted sex so much more than I have. From the very first I simply couldn't believe this man. Morning. Noon. Night. Anytime. All the time.

"Well, you probably know what happened. It wasn't long until I began to resent his pressures. He wasn't thinking of me. He was using me. So the more he pushed, the more I withdrew, and finally things started going downhill. Fast. That was so sad, because we really do love each other.

"Then one day the Lord gave me this simple little prayer. I can't tell you how often I've prayed it. But I can tell you for sure this one simple little prayer has changed our sex life completely. I mean a one-hundred-eighty-degree turn-around. And this is the prayer:

"*'Lord, help me make it memorable for him.'*

"I think what happened is that when I asked the Lord to make it memorable for my husband, my husband tried harder to make it memorable for me. So then another wonderful thing happened. I began to enjoy our mutual giving until would you believe? I've come to the place where I think sex is simply super! And it all started with that one little prayer:

"'Lord, help me make it memorable for him.'"

• • •

Positions, techniques, approaches, information, data—they're all important. But what is most important?

One answer:

When souls relate to the maximum,

Then bodies celebrate to the maximum

• • •

Prayer: O Divine Creator, we believe we were made by you for every kind of blending with each other: soul, mind, body. Help us first to blend with you that we "twain shall become one flesh." So may we, with you, celebrate our love in your love.

Amen

THE GIFT OF MONEY MANAGEMENT

Another formula for happy marriage*
Give ten percent
Save ten percent
Spend the rest with
thanksgiving and praise

• • •

Happy is the couple who can reach a blended formula for:

spending

saving

giving

for they will be far ahead of the crowd

What crowd? That miserable crowd fussing and fretting, nit-picking and moaning, "Where have all the dollars gone?"

Anyone who traffics much with husbands and wives soon comes on familiar problem points. And one of these is sure to be dollars and cents, bills and family finances, plus general economics.

Two histories here, two sets of tendencies. Two kinds of attitudes and behold all those habits of all those years crying out for blending.

What will we do with these? If we are wise, we will discuss and discuss and discuss. Then we will pray.

---

*Editor's note: The Abundance Foundation, established by the Shedds early in their writing career, receives fifty percent of their income for agricultural missions. Grants have been made to more than twenty-five animal projects around the world. Goats and water buffalo for the Philippines; mules in Thailand; dairy herds at a leper colony in Korea and in Zaire; chickens for Ghana and India; pigs for Haiti. In our own country a major project has been providing animals for Presbyterian Training Center, a farm for retarded teenagers in Virginia.

Always it's been true in our marriage—

the more we pray together

the more intelligently we can

give

save

spend the rest with thanksgiving and praise

• • •

Question for the dollars and a growing good sense:

Month by month and year by year

do our paychecks represent mostly worry,

mostly blessing?

Scripture symposium for meditation together:

"When thou hast eaten and art full, and hast built goodly houses, and dwelt therein, beware thou forget not the Lord thy God. . . . If I have made gold my hope or said to the fine gold, Thou art my confidence, I have denied the God above. . . . Labor not to be rich, for riches make themselves wings; they fly away as an eagle. . . . Lay not up for yourselves treasures in heaven. For where your treasure is there will your heart be also. . . . He which soweth sparingly shall reap also sparingly; and he which soweth bountifully shall reap bountifully. . . . All things come of thee, O Lord, and of thine own do we give to thee."*

BLESSING OF THE HAPPY SURPRISES

APPRECIATION OF THE LITTLE THINGS

THE GIFT OF LISTENING

---

*Selections in this Scripture symposium are from various translations of: Deuteronomy 8, Proverbs 23, Job 31, Matthew 6, 2 Corinthians 9, and 1 Chronicles 9.

DELAYED BLESSING FROM THE HARD THINGS

THE GIFT OF CERTAINTY

THE BLESSING OF SIMPLICITY

THE GIFT OF ADVENTURE

THE BLESSING OF SEX AT ITS MAXIMUM

THE GIFT OF MONEY MANAGEMENT

Put them all together, who wouldn't want all these blessings, these gifts of prayer? And this is His promise: He is waiting to bless us "far more abundantly than all that we ask or think" (Ephesians 3:20).

There's that word again, "WAIT!"

Why do we hear it over and over? To which comes the same monotonous answer—spiritual growth is slow, slow, slow. So many of the Lord's good things only seem to arrive by oxcart over the hill or by late canoe through the backwaters; long, long delay. But one day if we are faithful, the blessings do come, the gifts arrive. No trumpets. No advance notice. Things are simply better. We like each other more. We're having a happier time together. Our love is of new quality. Is this what the Quakers mean by their pensive phrase "I felt the evil in me weakened and the good raised up"?

• • •

Fact:

Any couple who will commit themselves to pray together and stay with it over the years—will be in for blessings today, blessings tomorrow, but especially blessings far off in their future. The reason? At its apex, Christian prayer for the married is two lovers together becoming a channel for God's love to flow both *to* them and *through* them.

"Plant patience in your heart. The roots may be bitter, but the fruit will be sweet."

Ancient saying
and Anonymous

Chapter X

Fruit of the Spirit

"The fruit of the spirit is love, joy, peace, longsuffering, gentleness, goodness, faith, meekness, temperance."

Galatians 5:22–23 (KJV)

TESTS FOR SPIRITUAL GROWTH*

Most of us like to be called "a good egg." Your father and mother probably remember watching someone candle eggs at their grocery store. Your grandpa and grandma have seen it for sure.

The grocer would sit on a stool or stand behind the counter. Then he would take a small box with a hole on top; inside there was a candle or light bulb. Each egg brought in by the farmer's wife would be carefully lifted and held over the hole to make certain this was a good egg. Against the light, bad eggs showed plainly.

Galatians 5:22 and 23 make up what we call the great egg candler of the Bible. By these verses we can test any teaching, any group, any movement, and the church. It's the same for us individually. And the passage will do for couples too.

"The fruit of the spirit is love, joy, peace, longsuffering, gentleness, goodness, faith, meekness, temperance."

Important note:

The word is "fruit," not "fruits." Love, joy, peace are God's doing, not ours. These are by-products of our life with Him. And because this is true, we must be constantly checking.

Here are the nine test questions we developed together

---

*These tests for the real thing in spiritual growth appeared in *Celebration in the Bedroom.* Although this book deals especially with body communication, we developed these nine tests many years ago as tests for the real thing in every area of our relationship. We have found them particularly revealing as we continually examine our prayer life together.

from Galatians 5:22–23. They constitute for us a biblical, foolproof test of whether our prayer life is authentic.

– 1 –

"The fruit of the spirit is *love*."

Is there an increasing concern for each other in our marriage?

More and more do we really care what our mate thinks, feels?

Are we growing in our "otherness"?

More words for "love" that we have found in various versions:

charity . . . caring . . . concern . . .

solicitude . . . devotion . . .

– 2 –

"The fruit of the spirit is *joy*."

Are there increasing seasons of gladness in our relationship?

Are there more and more times when we sense the glow of real happiness; when we plain feel good together?

Other possibilities:

Jubilance . . . cheerfulness . . .

elation . . . laughter . . . mirth . . .

– 3 –

"The fruit of the spirit is *peace*."

Is there an increasing quiet in our hearts, in our home, in our love?

As time passes are we truly more content, relaxed?

Other possibilities:

serenity . . . composure . . .

harmony . . . repose . . .

tranquillity . . . stillness . . .

– 4 –

"The fruit of the spirit is *longsuffering*."

Is there an increasing stretch in our attitudes?

Do the little oddities in each other and in all others disturb us less?

Are we more patient? More even-tempered?

Jesus stood for something, and we will too. We do not want to become so broad that we flatten out into "anything goes." But even when we must disagree, can we do so with a greater appreciation of the other person's rights?

Additional possibilities:

forbearance . . . flexibility . . .

tolerance . . . adaptability . . .

– 5 –

"The fruit of the spirit is *gentleness*."

Are we increasingly kind, more courteous, softer in our touch?

Physically, mentally, verbally, are we more tender?

Longsuffering deals with our attitude toward those things people do to us. This question asks the opposite: Are we more Christlike in the things we do to other people?

Added possibilities:

docile . . . soothing . . . compassionate . . .

mellow . . . gracious . . .

"The fruit of the spirit is *meekness*."

Is there a growing self-honesty in each of us?

From the many interpretations of meekness, we have worked out our own definition:

"True meekness is to know the difference between what we are right now and what God intends us to be."

For us, closing these gaps is one more goal of great marriage.

"Measure us, Lord. Keep measuring us."

Other possibilities:

mildness ... humility ...

yielding ... resignation ... submission ...

"The fruit of the spirit is *goodness*."

More and more do we seek to be a blessing?

Do we reach out to help others beyond our own address? Are we making an honest effort out there to do something good, to say something kind, to lift?

There is a goodness that counts itself good, because it isn't bad. But Christian goodness is never inert. It doesn't hold back in the face of need, nor hesitate to act for the public welfare.

Other possibilities:

ministry ... helpfulness ...

generosity ... service ...

— 8 —

"The fruit of the spirit is *faith.*"

These fears of ours, are they on the decline?

Do we worry less, trust more?

Do we really believe there is a power greater than our own?

When we are anxious, are we better able to share our anxieties with each other and trust the Lord?

Additional possibilities:

reliance . . . belief . . .

confidence . . . assurance . . .

— 9 —

"The fruit of the spirit is *temperance.*"

Are we more and more in charge of our emotions?

Are we growing in that kind of self-control that is truly Christ-control, poised with His poise?

If the Spirit of the Lord is really at work in us, we should rattle less, scatter less, crater less. Is this how it is with us?

Other possibilities:

self-restraint . . . self-rule . . .

self-mastery . . . self-discipline . . .

• • •

Anyone pondering these test questions will realize again that pacing is all-important. Great marriage does not come by the chance matching of two horoscopes. The love divine for couples is never "spin the wheel and wish us luck." Galatians 6:9 says, "In due season we shall reap if we faint not." Praying together is more like that.

Chapter XI

Question Time

Questions, questions, all kinds of questions. They come by phone, by mail, in personal consultation. And especially they come during our *Fun in Marriage* workshops. In each of the three sessions—Vocal, Body, and Soul Communication—we have a period called "Question Time." Some of the questions come directly from the floor, but most of them come via a written note.

In this chapter we deal with the six questions most often asked at "Question Time."

How does your prayer together fit into family devotions? Isn't it important also to teach the whole family how they can communicate with the Lord?

It certainly is important. Vital. Today's young desperately need a vertical reference. Family devotions can be exactly that for them.

What constitutes a praying family? When our children were small, we settled on four goals:

I.   A fun family devotion time
II. Mother and father praying together
III. Each person in the family having a personal quiet time
IV. Every member of the family praying daily for every other member

After numerous tries and failures we arrived at this format for our family devotions:

Our evening meal begins with "Most Interesting Things." When everyone is in place at the table, we ask this question, "What was the most interesting thing that happened to you in the past twenty-four hours?" Now come the reports. Fascinating. Some glad, some sad, some whimsical, some from faraway places in the soul.

Several good things are taking place here. Every person is opening the door a bit for all to see inside. Result? We are coming to know each other, understand each other, appreciate each other. We are also learning by sharing together that God has packed each day with special blessings. Any hour, any moment He may surprise us.

When we have finished the first round of "Interesting Things," we usually go the second round or a third. By the time we have finished, dinner is almost over. Then follows Bible reading. If preferred, the leader (we take turns leading) may bring some favorite from elsewhere. A devotional book, someone's writing on prayer, even a secular magazine. *Teen, Sports Illustrated, Newsweek, Reader's Digest,* and many others have come to our table.

Books, too, and some of these may be eyebrow raisers. Such as? Such as *The Psychic Experiences of Dogs and Cats.* That one was good for several weeks.

Finally the session closes with a summary prayer by this day's leader. Another good time with our "Fun Family Devotions" has brought its blessings.

Addenda Question:

Honestly, now, did you do this every night, every dinner time?

The answer has to be yes, no, yes.

Yes, we almost always had Interesting Things.

No, we didn't always include the Bible reading.

Yes, we always closed with prayer—the Lord's Prayer . . . silent prayer . . . perhaps even Dad's plain vanilla, "The Lord knows we're busy tonight. We will each of us pray on the way."

This was our finding: Family devotions, to continue with any semblance of regularity, must be a happy time; each member of the family must be given a chance to participate; and the entire event must be relaxed, interesting, fun.

Addenda Question Two:

At what age should we start family devotions?

Answer: Very, very early. Adapted and tailored for the smallest child, the results will be surprising. Even the little ones soon catch on to "Interesting Things," and they love it.

You say praying on our knees can bring special blessing to our marriage. Why?

For one thing it's humbling. Together on our knees we seem to see our faults more clearly and we also find them easier to admit. Because this is true, praying on our knees has a way of closing gaps and healing wounds.

Then too if we ever prayed on our knees in childhood, praying on adult knees may take us back with warm recall. (Interesting sidelight: Some women tell us that even a reluctant husband may respond to the simple invitation, "Will you kneel with me by our bed? I need to talk with the Lord and I need you to share this time with me.")

One surprised wife who attended a *Fun in Marriage* workshop sent this report some time later.

Her husband, she said, had never prayed with her except occasionally at mealtimes. Then one night she invited him to kneel by her side while she prayed. And he did. In fact, she said, he did it again, and again, and then again. Now here comes the punch line:

"Rodney is a football coach. Big jock type and proud of his image. But one night recently when I knew he was hurting bad, real bad, he said a simple prayer for God to help him. He really prayed. You can imagine how I felt, and I'm sure you can imagine too what I think this might mean for our future."

– 3 –

*We know from our reading of BIBLE STUDY TOGETHER
that you two have read through the Bible many times together.
Would you tell us about your other reading?*

We recommend that any couple interested in spiritual
growth begin right now building their own library of prayer
books. Where to begin? For starters try the Christian
Bookstore. Browse for that particular "this one is for us"
feeling. We all have specialized needs and particular reading
that touches us.

The mystics of the Middle Ages have been a special
blessing to our prayer life. Readers of *Bible Study Together*
will know of our "candles, arrows, and question marks."
These we developed first for Bible study but we also use the
same three marks in other reading. We think they are
particularly good in the self-help literature. Psychology,
psychiatry, anything that shows us where we've come from
can be a real plus.

Is it dangerous to be each other's counselors, each other's
psychiatrists? Not if we're praying together.

Do you ever become confused with all the different terms for God? Almighty, Heavenly Father, Divine Creator, Jesus, Holy Spirit, and all the others in preaching and song are really hard to sort out. Recently our preacher had a series on the Trinity. Talk about a muddle. After hearing the whole series, I had one question, "What is the Trinity?"

We believe couples praying together do well to discuss these things and sort out what they can of theology. Then let them select that name for deity which feels right for them. Our preference is "The Lord." We also have strong feelings for the Quaker term, "The Inner Presence." Whatever and however we name His Name, our Jewish friends did a great thing for all of us. That was a classic moment when they inscribed on believers' hearts for all time:

THE LORD OUR GOD IS ONE GOD

– 5 –

We have never mastered the discipline of intercessory prayer. It is so easy to say, "I'll be praying for you," but for us, it's even easier to forget to pray like we said we would.

We know of no better answer than the prayer list, the prayer notebook, the prayer journal. Of these three, the journal may be especially helpful. Here we can list the people we're praying for, the situations we're praying about, all kinds of needs. Some of these may be in short hand; dated at their entries; brief notes; just enough to be reminders.

When we feel a particular prayer has been answered, we write a brief description and date that too. This kind of record, kept together, can make for a wonderful diary of mutual growing in the Lord.

If God already knows our needs, why pray?

No one could give a complete answer to the "Why pray?" question in a few words. Since it's such a good question, it makes an ideal research project for the married. Always, finding our own answers is sure to be a positive for couples praying together.

Yet doesn't the question, as it is asked here, consider only one side of prayer? We recently heard a father in one of our workshops talk about the other side:

"When one of my children says, 'Dad, I need your help,' that makes me feel so fine.

"But here is another twist I think you should tell teenagers. My fifteen-year-old has taken to asking, 'Dad, what can I do for you?'

"Now that is something else, isn't it? I've been thinking about this and about God and us as his children. I used to think we only prayed to get what we want from God. Now I'm beginning to see that prayer is so much more than asking. Sure, He promised to bless us, but doesn't He also like it when we want to bless Him?"

Chapter XII

Promise

At the conclusion of *Bible Study Together* we offered this absolute guarantee:

That couple who will keep the Scriptures central

in their relationship

By any method, ours, or one of their own making,

That couple, in even thirty days, will experience

positive changes in their love.

Now comes another promise, this one straight from the Lord Himself—

"Call to me and I will answer you:

I will tell you wonderful and marvelous

things."

Jeremiah 33:3 (Good News)

Other translators make *wonderful* and *marvelous*: "remarkable secrets" . . . "great mysteries" . . . "hidden things" . . . "joys of which you have no knowledge."

All of these from biblical scholars. And then the lingual experts add this veritable fantasmagoria:

"exciting surprises" . . . "incredible" . . . "thrilling vistas" . . . "awesome" . . . "things to shout about" . . . "to celebrate" . . . "limitless possibilities" . . . "the dream come true" . . . "truly divine."

So the more we study Jeremiah 33:3 word by word, the more it explodes with meaning.

Plus the more it comes clear that His "exciting surprises" and "things to shout about" do not come free. These gifts are not like some lucky number on some lucky card. These He gives us by His grace, but we must earn them by our efforts.

Every day we hear the many casual calls of routine living: . . . "Call me some time for coffee" . . . "I only called to say hello" . . . "Call and let me know when the meeting starts."

But in the original language the "call" of Jeremiah 33:3 is not at all casual. Here the meaning is "earnest calling, the call of commitment, the call of ongoing lifestyle."

This is the call to which He promises all the good bound up in "wonderful" and "marvelous."

So the secret is

    day by day

        week by week

            month by month

                and year by year

                    to call and keep on calling

How long?

Forty-seven years?

This is our witness and this is our experience—

For forty-seven years we have been studying the Bible together,

learning to pray together

and out of those forty-seven years

these things we know for sure:

    I. With or without prayer your forty-seven years are sure to pass anyway.

    II. If you will make your days and weeks and months a pilgrimage of tuning in upward together

The Lord Himself *will* one day bring you
where the blessed are—
and you will experience
your own unique and very special
heaven on earth with Him.